MY ODYSSEY

A journey of love, loss, loneliness, and light

Apoorva Ravi

Inkfeathers Publishing
www.inkfeathers.com

My Odyssey
by Apoorva Ravi
Paperback

First published in 2023 by
Inkfeathers Publishing, New Delhi 110095

ISBN 9789390882908

www.inkfeathers.com

I dedicate this book to all those people
who have been there for me
through good and bad times.

I thank all the people in my life who have inspired me. A special mention to my parents for being with me for 33 years, through the ups and downs of life.

Foreword

Chirasree Bose

Author of 4 Indian Fictions, Writer, Blogger, Editor

Love, loss, loneliness, and light—so beautifully in harmony with each other! I loved every bit of it. Apoorva's writing will touch your heart, and soon, you will see the beauty of rawness in it. I was hooked right from the first piece of poetry—so easily relatable. I personally, and strongly so, feel that we need books that we can relate to. Books should speak to us and be our solace. Apoorva's book will be that to you, as it has been for me for the past couple of days. It will bring to you how people feel in real life, their unfiltered vulnerabilities, their struggles with the need for love as well as the practicality of having to stay away from it, and so much more. Believe me as I say this: you're in for a realistic and pleasing journey through a woman's heartfelt words. I feel so honored to have gotten the opportunity to read this concise yet beautiful book before it could land in your hands.

To Apoorva: *All the best with the book. I loved your poetry and every little write-up in it. So honest and so relatable. Looking forward to its success!*

Chapter 1

Looking Back at the Past through the Lens of the Present

We often say that the past is something we have left behind. But we are mistaken. The past always catches up with the present. In fact, our past experiences shape our present.

Traces of my past mistakes are at times visible in my present flaws. And it's better to accept them than cry out and fret saying, 'I thought I have changed, But I am still the same.'

'We change from time to time
From past to present, present to future.
Life expects us to change.
We expect ourselves to change
To be a better version of ourselves

A version that we can look up to and smile.

But every version of the present is shaped by the past…

A mistake made in the past will impact our future.

The help we rendered in the past will show up as gratitude in the present.

So why not just accept our past?

As it's past experiences that determine our choices in the present and future.'

A Thursday Afternoon…

The cloudy sky is trying to swallow the sun, but I can still see the malevolent efforts of the sun, trying to send rays that fall on my face through my meshed window. But then again, the clouds cover the rays, and the sun finally decided not to fight but join hands with the rain-filled clouds and they are now jointly drawing the rainbow colors on the afternoon sky, eliciting a sense of calm in my turbulent thoughts.

These thoughts that I repeatedly have nowadays seem never-ending! Thoughts like 'Am I too selfish? Do I not care? Is that why he is not there with me right now? Because I didn't risk it to be with him? Do I love myself too much? Is it the reason why I can't leave my home and be with him and his mom?' cloud my head and just don't leave me!

A curled softness touched my feet. And my love, Olive, whipped my feet with his swishy tail, as he was coming to sleep on the laptop on my bed. Well, that's his favorite spot and he would be mighty displeased if I try to make him get up.

Yes, I have two cats Olive and Peach, and both of them

occupy significant space in my life. Then why do I need anyone isn't it? That's what I think too, but there are times when I yearn for his presence, whose logical mindset, though I want to crush, I also adore. I just want to ask him, why not at least once, just go with the flow?

Well, maybe it's difficult for him. Just as planning is difficult for me. And that's the reason for us to have not taken the step.

The Next Day…

Today is the day…

I have my first workshop at a school as part of my mental health initiative, Destigmatize. And ironically, I am experiencing the same thing which I am going to talk about at the workshop: how to manage stress.

Well, I am prepared and that ought to give me confidence, but self-doubt is a friend who doesn't say goodbye very quickly. And the familiar questions like 'Am I doing the right thing,' returned.

Chime, I receive a text from my mom, saying that my dress made me look intelligent and that my cats are fine. Ah, she knows very well how much I worry about my cats when I go out. And, whether I look intelligent or not, her message cheered me up. And the song 'Dream to Keep Us Going' by Easy Wanderlings started playing through my earphones, relaxing me.

Looking at the eager students at the workshop reminded me of my school days, those memories were happy, sad, and a mix of both. That's what life is right? It's grey.

'Bouncing up and down the bench.
To answer every question the teacher asked,
I sometimes forgot about my friends sitting all around me.
Lonely I became, traversing the obstacles of life,
Lacked a support system to fall back on...
But still, few people around me offered their unwavering support.
And that made me realize the power of the collective...
The value of being there for each other and not just trampling each other to get ahead in life!'

The children and their innocence are two things that I loved watching during the workshop and just hope that they retain some of it at least while navigating the mystery, which is life. Because life teaches individuals a lot of things, but in my case, I have never learned to step ahead and not delve into the past.

But the past has laid its impressions on the present. Let's revisit them to make sense of today.

Chapter 2

Swinging Back and Forth: My Tussle with Life

The Mirror

Life taught me many lessons. Different instances and unknown people are sometimes the best teachers…

In 2013, I was diagnosed with psychotic depression. The days were difficult, and challenging as I had to tussle with my emotions, my body, and my mind to stay in control.

It was on one such day that I saw myself in the mirror. I could not recognize myself. I saw a stranger whom I didn't want to identify with. I used to tell myself that I am not the fat person the mirror showed. I was instead, the dancer, athletic, vibrant, and full of life. I never used to connect with the zombie-like creature that I had become, who had to take antidepressants so that I could be deemed normal according to doctors.

With frequent fights with my mother, I found the terrace to be my safe haunt. I would remain there sometimes till 1 am at night.

And one evening at around 6 pm, I saw her.

She was dancing. And to me, she was an angel. She was not like those thin dancers but still, she looked so beautiful. She looked so happy. I was mesmerized.

It was then that I started to dance again and did not let the illness take my joy of moving to the beats of music.

Lemons or Lemonade?

Another question that used to bother me during those days was—why me?

It was then that I learnt: When life gives us lemons... we don't have to always turn them into lemonade, do we? Why not for once, enjoy the lemon as it is...

I learnt that my attempts of always trying to make lemonade out of lemon, caused me to push my emotions away that one day it burst out as psychosis.

Because during my masters the lemonade turned sour. Some might say it was not the best period of my life. But I would say it was a game-changer.

Life during that time taught me things that I had only dreamt of... Oh yes, the lessons were hard. The modality was way too harder. You will never guess but the modality was psychotic clinical depression. I was diagnosed with it and life turned topsy-turvy.

From writing gibberish in my exam answer script to saying sorry repeatedly to everyone... I was a mess...You must be thinking, what is the lesson that I have learnt? The lesson is something that I will never forget and is with me even now when

I feel low or high. It is that when you hit rock bottom, you develop courage you never knew you ever had. When you lose it all, there is nothing left to lose. It is then that you learn to accept life. Accept the lemon it offers you and enjoy it without turning it into lemonade.

'Seeking a Human Connection'

I realize now that 10 years have passed since my depressive breakdown at college. I can remember crying at college during my final examination. When I could hear the voices of my parents, friends, and teachers in my head. There were many intense emotions that were running through my mind at that time and one strong emotion was guilt. The guilt that I had got attached to my teacher. I knew it was brotherly, but I didn't know if others thought about it that way. I repeatedly said sorry to my friends and teacher in the exam hall.

Later I was taken to a doctor by my parents, a psychiatrist, who prescribed medications. My symptoms improved and I improved gradually, but the guilt remained...

Also, another emotion that arouse from the depths of this experience is the feeling of betrayal. My parents had to initially give me medicines without my knowledge, and I struggled hard with acceptance. And it is now, looking back at everything, I pen these lines:

'I have often struggled with acceptance.
Acceptance of my mental illness
Accept that it's ok to take medicines
Accept that it was initially given without consent

Accept that the doctor who broke it to me blamed me?
Accept that mental illness is still looked at with a diagnostic lens
Where the onus of recovery is on the person
Where the person is often blamed, and the caregivers pitied.
Yes, I struggle with it…
I struggle to accept that my struggle was kept a secret from the rest.
That I had only a few channels of outlet
And left at the mercy of medication and exercise?
They say to focus on work and improve yourself, be productive and rest will be fine…
But was being productive the end goal?
Wasn't my voice important?
They thought I was being stubborn,
But I was just coming to terms with myself.
'All mental health patients are initially reluctant, said the medical professionals.
But is force the solution?
Should people not be given time to reconcile with their situation?
Oh! but time is money, they said.
Time should not be wasted!
Lest your academic career is impacted, they told me. …
They cried, they pitied but were not empathetic…
They said they understand,

But did they really?

Not then, but maybe now yes

I am glad that they listened now,

Understood me and my situation

And gave me a space to heal.

A space to cry out

A space to just be me…'

With acceptance, the guilt receded too, and I still have retained contact with my teacher whom I respect a lot. But still, some aspect of the guilt was there, somewhere submerged, lurking in the background.

But then that day, when I shared my feelings of guilt with my therapist, the therapist just made a simple statement: 'You were just seeking a human connection.' And then, my guilt diminished.

And now, even after 10 years, I have retained that connection with my teacher, as a brother.

Fear

Why do we fear?

Because we fear losing.

We fear losing the people we love.

We fear losing ourselves.

We fear losing time.

And last, we fear life itself.

And here, I share my fear, I have a fear of what-ifs. Well, that's common, you may say but still, it's big, it's real and it's life crippling.

Because of this fear, I have missed enjoying moments, I have missed opportunities, I have missed a committed relationship, I have missed a lot. And let me tell you, that fear is still there, lurking in the corner, always ready to intrude on the most crucial moments of my life.

Life's Stamp Prints on Me: Understanding the Impact of Life Experiences on an Individual's Mental Health

My life experiences have impacted me in myriad different ways. Some have had positive influences, some negative, and some have had no impact at all, as I have just flowed through them like a river. Sometimes I wish that I would have just flowed through every experience of life, without letting it impact me. But that's not possible, is it?

Post a discussion with my therapist, I realized that we human beings do tend to find meaning in every experience of our life. And through this meaning-making process, we construct narratives: happy, sad, exciting, dark, and many more.

Sometimes, we do tend to take responsibility for the events in these experiences, which may be burnt in our memory forever. And it is here that we internalize the events in our lives and let them impact our present and the future. And to help you understand this, I will narrate a story.

Understanding The Stamp Prints of Experiences in My Life

When I was five years old, I had a dog. The dog and I were best friends. A few months later, after I fell sick, I could not find

Snoopy anymore. I was told by my mother that Snoopy had to go to its mother and I was pacified. But a few years later, my parents told me that they had to give Snoopy away because my doctor told them so. I was heartbroken. Did this experience stamp a print on me? Maybe yes or maybe not. But I have often wondered about it…

Another incident of my life that I significantly remember is one of my favorite cousin brothers (who is now dead) telling me that he would not share secrets with me anymore because I tend to share them with my mother and his. And this impacted me as well. Though he did not mean it seriously, I took it to heart and would always rethink it. So, whenever he would not talk to me, I would wonder, 'Is it because of what I did that day?'

And, during pre-school, some of my friends bullied me during the lunch hour. And I was led to believe that for people to like someone, they should do something for them. So, since I wanted to be included with friends as part of their group, I became a people-pleaser in my latter school days. Even in my college days, I would think that I had to help my friends, or else they would not be with me anymore.

Self-Learned Techniques to Deal with Emotions

But being a people pleaser would become tiresome, and I would then retreat into the cocoon of my books and diary. I started to not hang out with friends much after school and college and would focus only on my studies. Studying became a coping skill to not mingle with others.

And I used to think that I was unwanted, and these feelings intensified during my post-graduation, after my cousin's death, leading to anxiety, depression, and psychosis…

Unlearning and the Need for Therapy

Picking the pieces of my life after a psychiatric evaluation, I learned to unlearn my thought process and behavior patterns. From accepting that everything that happens in life is not my fault, to learning to not grow over-dependent on people who care, I started understanding myself better. Therapy helped and still helps me identify that I am not responsible for other people's emotions.

'Learn to express yourself' is a motto that I now strongly believe in. And through my podcasts and poems, I want to convey to people to build an inner circle of significant people in their life so that they can express their thoughts and emotions with them and not keep everything within. But of course, understanding others' boundaries is another valuable lesson that I learned. Because relationships can be nurtured and developed with healthy and dynamic boundaries between people. And, though life leaves its stamp prints on each one of us, 'Let your past not shadow your present or stunt your future.'

Non-linear Journey of Mental Health Recovery

Here, I am not talking about how I was diagnosed with mental illness, but it is about me trying to reflect on the why. And to be frank, the why isn't always there. And it is equivalent to the same "why" that we ask ourselves if we are diagnosed with a physical illness. We may find a justifiable reason, for both, and then weave a story for the outside world. But does the "why" for mental illness ever satisfy anyone at all?

Mental illness is often called—invisible illness. Because the illness is not visible. It's everything in the mind. And people like me, who are diagnosed with it are sometimes asked—is there no cure? Yes, there is. Both psychiatry and psychology have progressed extensively to help individuals cope with mental health issues. But one needs to understand that there is no magic pill that would help you recover from mental illness like the one you would take for a cough or cold. In fact, it's not even managed the same way that long-term physical illnesses like diabetes are managed.

Mental health recovery and its cyclic nature

I was diagnosed with psychotic depression in 2013. And my recovery has not been straightforward or linear. From having a psychotic breakdown in college to hearing voices and then recovering with medication and counselling, my 10-year journey has been long. And there were times when things would seem perfect, but I would be having mood swings the next day. So, I would ask myself sometimes, when will this end?

But it was only later that I realized: mental wellness and illness are cyclic and continuous processes. Our mind is like a pond that needs to be watered frequently and nourished.

Can the reduction of symptoms be equated with recovery?

I have seen people make a common statement, you were mentally unwell, but now you are fine, so you are completely cured, isn't it? But is the reduction of symptoms synonymous with a complete cure? And can there ever be a complete cure? This is a very subjective question owing to the vast number of concerns that people have. Some people may need therapy and some medication and some both. And remission is a slow process.

Some are asked to stop taking medications after prognosis and others are asked to take them on a protectionist basis, lifelong. And some others may seek therapy regularly for a while and then seek it again, whenever they need it. So, it's always on a case-by-case basis and there is no one size fits all.

Hence, though I have reiterated many things that are commonly known, I find that a lot of people are still unaware of the facets of mental health. And to be fair on people, mental health, illness, and wellness form a very broad topic, and no one can say that they know everything about it. Yet, as we move towards a more aware and progressive society, it's time we try to gain an understanding of the layers of mental health, because who knows, it may help you understand yourself and others better.

Mental Wellness

Based on my observations of my mental health journey, I have often wondered what can be done to offer mental health support in society. And during one such introspection with self, the question of what my earliest childhood memory is popped up.

And things like me playing on the slide outside of school and waiting for my mother to pick me up or me waiting on the windowsill in the evening, waiting for my father to return from the office came to my mind. This habit continued for a long and later I grew up. But my special connection with my parents has remained the same.

Even now, when I am 32 years old.

I share all my ideas, wins, and joys with them, yes you guessed it right—they are one of my significant people. I also have a circle of few friends, a teacher cum brother, cousins, and a lovely aunt.

I do share my thoughts with them too. I do consult them on matters that bother me, and they do consult me as well when they want. I am privileged to have access to a supportive space, but still, I did get depression during my college. All these people were there then too, but I had disconnected from them or mainly was not expressing myself clearly to them or myself. I created a cycle of fear and assumptions that led to a diagnosis of depression. Of course, the disconnection was part of the depression itself. It was to an extent not in my hands then. But maybe I would have gained therapy and support faster if I had been able to identify the signs. Many psychologists and psychiatrists say that mental health service users are reluctant and refuse therapy and treatment initially. But why is it so? People do not resist treatment for arthritis or diabetes. It's probably because the literature and content available on mental health are limited and there is a high level of stigma associated with it.

What if it is taught in schools and colleges to every student at a basic level? What if the importance of Emotional well-being and not just intelligence is emphasized by society and the education system? Then perhaps people will more easily identify the signs themselves and seek medical attention quickly.

The onus of sound mental health is not only on psychologists and psychiatrists. It's on us, the society. We need to bring systemic changes—at both policy and societal levels and also the individual level to see a significant change. We need to have more and more conversations about it in the living room, parties, and workspaces and not just restrict it to the mental health professional's couch. We, as a society, should be there for each other, and then that perhaps will bring a minuscule degree of change in the mental health domain, where a lot of work needs to be done.

My Life Choices

'You are divergent, you are confused, you are so unfocussed' was a common phrase I have used to hear. And I would sometimes roll into a ball of self-doubt or cringe with irritation as to why can't people let me be. The questions people asked about my decisions made me question myself and complicate the situation even more.

And especially when I left two jobs in a row, these questions were more, and I cried out to my mother and father, that people are so judgmental. It was then that they told me that they had my back and that I didn't have to worry about anything else.

I feel I didn't value those words then, but I do now. It's so important to have the support of your parents. And I have now spread my wings wide like a bird, but the anchors are my parents.

Career Chaos

Further talking about my impulsiveness and divergent thoughts, I have observed that there are quite a few like me. So, for those who are impulsive and make decisions when they are impulsive, here's a small snapshot of me and my career choices.

If you look at my career graph of having not taken an IT job after engineering to doing a master's in mass communication with a stint in the industry as a writer and later having worked as a communication professor and starting PhD followed by my own social initiative, destigmatize; you would see divergence or diverse experiences. The choice is yours to make. And I look at it through different lenses too, depending on my mood and the situation.

Aside from calling oneself impulsive, a positive way to

describe oneself would be that you are driven by passion and act upon your dreams with passion.

But many times, people have asked me, 'What do you really want?' And to answer this question, I have taken time to understand and accept myself. There is a part of me that gets bored of things easily when I lose that passion.

But it is not that I have lost interest in them if they are really significant in my life. For example, you can look at my pattern with my PhD. I was really passionate about it when I started, but somewhere down the line the difficulties and the challenges of academic writing got to me, and I felt that a PhD is something I am not interested in anymore.

Yet, that's not true because I have time and again gotten back to it and worked on it quite hard. So, my interest in the topic is prevalent. I have observed that I have moments of intense passion towards it then reduced interest and then again increased passion. So, I have decided to do something about my behavior pattern. I have decided that during those moments of intense passion, I will work on it. And during the disinterest phase, I won't pressure myself because I might feel like quitting. I just need to do other stuff and then get back to it.

So, this is just an example to emphasize that for me and people like me, who are driven by passion, you need to know what are those things that are really significant and important in your life. And for those things, it's essential to give yourself time when you feel like giving up. Tell yourself to take a break and not give up because later your passion will be back, and you will work on it with deep interest and happiness. Here's a poem to remind the meandering souls out there about the significance of important things in life:

Apoorva Ravi

The Familiar Notes

When the wind was blowing me astray
The familiar notes, they got me home
I was lost, and wondering where to go...
But then I heard it.
The beats of comfort,
The lyrics tinted with wisdom,
they led me to my path,
The tunes of melody gave direction to my broken chords
And every word of those notes gave meaning to my incomplete thoughts.
Helping me see familiarity in my unfamiliar life.

Chapter 3

A Journey Towards Love

Him

I always wonder if it would have been different if I didn't have a mental illness. Would it have worked between us?

But, that itself was one of the reasons we connected so well... So, that, what if, should be thrown out of the window.

So let me introduce you to him.

I was always yearning for the person whose eyes and my eyes would get locked, and we would get lost together, but when that happened, I wasn't ready for it.

Now when I recollect the first time I met him,

I was nervous yet I called him. His profile seemed interesting. Jodi 365 was a reliable app indeed. It had matched me with a compatible person, and I didn't end up with some boy of my caste, like other apps… This was something that had been refreshing to talk to him about.

And from the first hello, where I just loved the baritone in his voice to the initial awkwardness, Or the time when I told him during our first meet that I had psychotic depression, and his acceptance, I just really love everything about us or the 'us' that we were.

And, as I think back to the time when I had not met anyone romantically, he was everything that I had dreamt about.

I don't know what love is. But on a sad day, if he calls, everything seems ok. When I hear his voice, I feel at home, and when I meet him, I feel relaxed.

But the question is, what is it that I love about him? It's the conversations we share, and the understanding that we have about each other that help us connect with each other. I remember the first time I met him, with masks on since it was during the Pandemic. Yes, it was a testing time, and I am grateful for his presence in my life during those months. I told him I had depression, the first time I met him, and it did not and does not matter to him to date. It's my uncertainty, my impulsiveness, my indecisiveness, and maybe his rigidity at that time that impacted the relationship. And it's only here that I wish my past relationships had not scarred me and I could have taken that leap of faith with him. Yet, then again, should only the girl take the leap of faith, or should he also have taken that leap? Still, both could not because of our own circumstances, and now it's the end, or is it?

And as I reminisce about the past, here are some poems on my expression of love and some on life.

Every song I listen to is about you.

But I fear taking the step to come to you...

Because I am not sure if you want me to
You say you are happy alone.
But that's my line.
And now I steal your line, what will you do when you are old?
Yes, you will be running a marathon.
But won't you want me by your side love?
I fool myself that I can grow old with someone else...
But that's not possible...
And let me tell you something...
I don't want a kiss from you!
But all I need is you.
All I want is you
All I Dream of is you…

*****

Burnt Bridges to Reach You

Burnt all bridges on the way, to reach you...
You seem the right fit, and there's no turning back.
There's no plan B, other than me and you...
For our goal and purpose to align
Our values sync and there's no reason to decline...
But have I done the right thing, in putting faith in us?
It's scary to not have an alternative bus.
To traverse life's journey through sun and dew...

I have put my complete trust in nobody but us two...

But what if I am not able to reach you or your path changes?

Well, I have given the reigns of the decision to time

And its ticking decides our fate.

Because only time can tell if the gamble was worth it...

For only time has the power to take me to you or away from you...

Single, In A Relationship, And Married

We commonly use the term, single, married, or 'in a relationship' to refer to people. But aren't we everything of the above-mentioned titles, in some way or the other? We are born, single, and die single; we are in a relationship with friends and family and perhaps married to our passion or purpose, and some others are married to a person legally too.

So, as I traverse through my multiple titles of being single, 'in a relationship with friends and family,' and married to my purpose, I find life very liberating. I work on research papers till late in the night and work on my social initiative, Destigmatize, to enable mental health awareness. I am also part of a community called, Warriors-Connect, where I have found my tribe.

And during one weekly huddle of Warrior's Connect, the talk on grief and loneliness which some of the people were experiencing, got me thinking. It made me realize the value of my parents, friends, my boyfriend, and brother cum mentor. They have all been supporting me and I am lucky for their support. The discussion also got me prepared for the eventuality of losing someone I love. So, being single is not a deterrent, yes sometimes one may feel lonely, but it is during those times that one should reach out to their friends, family, or community for support.

And so, my learning is that we all encounter, love, loss, and loneliness, and the cycle repeats itself, and it's important to be patient with ourselves and the world and take things one step at a time.

Poetry

My Lyrical Reflections of Life

The girl who reads romance novels

The girl who reads romance novels
The boy who makes logical lists
Had struggles in their relationship.
They broke up and patched up an unhealthy pattern...
It exhausted them both, but is it toxic that they broke up multiple times,
Or is it poignant that they still are there for each other during difficult times?
It's the perspective.
The way you see it matters...

What do I love?

I yearn not only for people but significant conversations,
Conversations where I can be an equal participant,
For conversations where I am neither dominant nor dominated…
For conversations with dynamic and mutual boundaries,
But not many that the beauty of the conversation is lost,
I realized something today, as I spoke to my therapist, and later in a group discussion,
What do I seek?
I seek to have meaningful conversations with people,
And through those conversations, find my sense of belonging...
I told my therapist today that sometimes, some conversations trigger my fear of abandonment…

But it's those conversations that lead me to question
myself and break my self-created walls of fear and
judgement,
I see the power in conversations,
Conversations that show us that we have multiple facets:
We can be having a therapeutic conversation about our
past loneliness,
And later be a part of a group conversing about the
challenges of a safe space.
And that leads to a question, what is a safe space?
Where there is no judgement? But is it even possible?
I fathom…
Is a safe space my self-created comfort zone?
Where only I decide what's to be said?
Is a safe space a utopia, where one can do and say whatever
they want?
And here, I ask, is what I love, even the right question?

Musings on Life

I like to move from places
Not stay put anywhere...
I like to flow like the river,
Running past the moments of life.
Eventually, I turn into an ocean,
Welcoming you into my arms.

But don't hesitate oh dear,
As you ride along the waves with me.
Life is nothing but a journey,
Where it takes minutes for moments to turn into memories...
Yes, it's true darling,
That you and I will soon be memories!

Imprint on My Soul

Your imprint on my soul is like the clay imprints I made when young...
Reminding me of childhood when I was carefree and innocent,
Molding clay with my fingers and deciding the depth of the imprint...
But now it's different...
It's not in my hands!
Your imprint on my soul is deeper than I ever imagined...
Which cannot be washed away by the waves of stormy nights or pleasant sunshine...

White Petals

White Petals, dancing to the tunes of the breeze.
My mind drifts to the times of happy memories...
Of the weekend meetings,
Of the shared kisses,
Of the tea parties from Chai Point,
With Samosas and Croissants to please our hunger.
But little did they know that they never did their job…
Because our hunger for each other ran much deeper!

At the Moment

I feel alive at this moment
With the beauty of life before me.
I am content.
I see my cats playing before me, chasing each other…
It makes me feel a fuzzy feeling of warmth and happiness.
A feeling of coziness envelopes me, I don't know why…
But maybe everything need not have a reason,
Everything we do, need not lead to something…
Life is happening and we need to appreciate it, at the moment...

Take that First Step

In life, we hesitate to go ahead…
We will always remain where we are.
Take that first step
Because once you do take the leap
You will be rewarded with untold surprises,
And treated to experiences that make the risk worthwhile…
But, as the dream-like experience of risks begins to give you the heady surge of thrill and happiness,
Do not forget reality and get stunned when it comes crashing down on you!

Beauty

What is beauty?
Is it that which we capture with our camera?
Or that which we capture through our eye
Or that which we perceive with our mind…
Difficult to say.
For sometimes, the rawness of nature in places like tea plantations is beyond beautiful.
Beautiful to the travelers who pass by
But reality tells a different story, a story of hard labor, a story of poverty, a story of deforestation, a story of loss…
There are multiple versions of every story, which can be unraveled only with time…

Letter to My Lover

You entered my Space,
You intersected with my thoughts,
Poured your emotions into my melting pot.
Which, I devoured willingly…
We tried to be a version of ourselves that would appeal to others….
But we failed.
We failed to reach the midpoint.
We broke up and patched up multiple times…
With each fall and rise, I was introduced to a different facet of you and you to mine…
You saw me for what I am, a set of broken glass pieces…
I saw you for what you are, wounded…
I wanted to try to understand…
I wanted to help you heal…
But you refused to pick the broken pieces of my soul…

The Parting

I am tired, he said.
And I knew that the end was near…
The end of a period that felt like a roller coaster ride...
A period of bittersweet memories…
End of a journey of friendship and understanding...
Alas! I wish it could have remained that way.
but the expectations were there from both ends...
Expectations that became bigger than us...

Chords of Life

A chord that's in tune, a chord that's off-key...

That's the true definition of life, isn't it?

Our lives are not a perfect symphony of music and lyrics...

Life instead, is like a jazz performance,

Where different instruments resound to produce music that may seem celebratory, melancholy, or something in-between...

And this in-between is the true pulse of life.

Because life is never this or that,

It's never in tune or off-key...

But instead, it always lies in between!

Yesterday Was Blue

Yesterday was not what it should have been…
Yesterday was blue...
But why cry today when you can see a bright hue?
Of sunshine flirting with the morning dew...
Reminding you that life is not all about bliss or blues,
But it is about taking solace from the comfort of loved
ones and venturing into the dance of life,
Taking risks, blowing chances, and living as nobody knew!

Half-Read Books

Half-read books, half-written stories
Incomplete me, incomplete you
My poems lack something...
Is it your rhythm that I miss?
When my words sync with your tune...
Is it music to the ear?
But whose ear is the question…
Your ears or mine...
Or of the world outside?
Isn't it strange that we try to fit our music into pre-existing templates?
Why should our music resemble anything that is the norm...
Why should sounds from you and me conform?
Why can't we make our own rules and then break them too...

Happiness is Not Momentary

Happiness is not momentary,
It's something to remember when
You wallow in depths of sadness,
Self-doubt and self-judgement...
When you are happy with yourself,
Why worry about what others say?
Why worry about what others think?
Why care if others judge you or not?

Life

Life is a journey that makes sense,
Only if one stays in the present…
Not delve into the past, nor ponder about the future...

Live Your Life

Live your life by being alive every minute...
Someone told me, don't be scared to get angry.
Don't be worried when you are too sad.
Because it just means you experience emotions strongly…
So, you will be too happy and too joyous as well...
Isn't that a wonderful thing?
To experience our emotions and live them to the fullest?
So, here's something I have to say to you all,
Don't be afraid, let that tissue get drenched in tears.
And let that clenched fist hit that wall,
Let your laughter echo to the world at large.
Do not be scared,
Do not be scared to let out,
Do not hold on, but just express.
Emotions need to see light.
And not be buried under darkness!

Slow Down

Slow down, the sun is not running away,
Tomorrow the rays will be back to greet you.
And till then you have the moonlight for company,
Do not be misled by the dimness
For moonlight guides you during the dark
At places where the sun is scared to enter…
Slow down, take a deep breath.
Did you know you can slow dance under the moonlight?
It's the time when you can unravel and be yourself…
So, don't go chasing those rays of brightness.
Be comfortable with the dimness too...
And you will be rewarded with brightness the next day.

Reborn

She looked around...
She wanted to make them happy,
She wanted to make them proud,
More importantly, she thought if she did, she would be loved!
That was the thought of the girl,
Who ran amok, finding ways, failing...
Yet finding another way to make them proud.

She picked up all the chips on the way,
Assembled them one on top of the other,
And tried to make the best of what she could...
But as the pressure hit the chips,
The chips started falling away...
As the chips fell away, her inner core was all that remained,
And she was reborn.

Why do we rely?

Why do we rely?
Because we know that when we cry,
They are there by our side,
They are the people we trust.
To help put faith back in ourselves when we mistrust.
They are our tribe.
And we will find them, in the most unexpected places.
They may always not say yes to appease.
But will be there to support us when we need.
And when do we need them?
Each one of them knows their time, their need.

Questions

I sometimes question myself.
Question my actions
Question my thoughts
Question my motives
Question my purpose
Question my work
Question my existence
But then, where do the questions end and where do the answers begin?
They say questions are good.
Stay Hungry, Stay Foolish
But how many questions are optimal?
Can questions not destabilize countries?
Can questions not destabilize societies?
Yes
Is it necessary?
Again Yes
And why yes?
The answer lies in the question.

Self Judgement Trap

We feel it's essential to justify.
When people say we are wrong
But we need to pause and think…
Do we really owe them an apology or a justification?
Isn't it just their perspective that we are wrong?
Do we even reflect upon our own perspective when judged…?
People think through their lens and unknowingly dismiss us….
Don't fall into the self-judgment trap, when people state their point of view, you just fight to have your own!

You

Why do you say I don't write about you?
When my every word is written thinking about you...
Don't think it's an exaggeration...
Nowadays I even get angry only because of you...
But the people around me, like my parents, are poor victims of my wrath...
I think about how to lead a happy life with you...
I understand I come with baggage and so do you...
But can we not reduce our load by sharing it and carrying it jointly?
We don't know what the future entails...
But one thing I know is true.
That in my future there exists a place that cannot be filled by anyone but you...
Yes, I do wear my heart on my sleeve.
But I bear my deepest thoughts and secrets with only some like you...
So, let's not worry, let's bare our souls, let's be raw and let's bring out the best and worst in me and you...

Go With the Flow

Why is it that we do say, Go with the flow…
But never follow it?
Why do we stop?
Why do we not go out there and do what we feel?
Why not, for once, not put filters over our emotions…
Not let our brain condition our heart…
Why?
What are we scared of?
Why do we restrict ourselves?

Why do we hinder our today with reflections of the past?
And console ourselves that we will do it tomorrow…
A tomorrow which will never arrive?
Why not just let go for once?
And set our emotions free?
For they are emotions…
Not wine, to get better when kept in a bottle.
For years together…

The Beach in My Backyard

Walking under the sky, the beauty
Chasing my dreams, I felt it:
The water under my feet
It was raining.
It was then that I felt it, the beach in my backyard
The solace of peace, calming,
like waves in a sea, crashing
Perfect harmony, its music
I was at peace, in eternal bliss.

Don't have to go anywhere, no, no, nowhere, but there
where the backyard gave me the beach feels
The right balance of bliss
Calming my insides and outside, like a musical symphony
Oh life, I love you, you teach lessons every day, I learn them.
Never felt so happy, like a sea wave kissed me under the sun.

Different Tunes Do Coexist

I realize that my low key can complement your high,
And both of us can make music that's unique.
A unique sound that may be off-key to some
But who cares?
As long as we continue to make music that's ours?
And learn to get better, one step at a time!
Music is not born melodious,
It's created with love and passion
And nurtured with patience and understanding.
Only then does it become a soulful symphony
And pleasing to the ears of everyone in our company!

Slow Dance Under Moonlight

I don't know where I will go.
I don't know where you will go...
But tonight, just slow dance with me under the moonlight
Tomorrow is another day, our destinations unknown...
But tonight, in your arms, I feel home is right here under the moonlight...
I do not know you, nor do you know me.
But tonight, the stars are whispering a magical melody for both of us to dance till eternity under the moonlight...
We may have our share of sorrows; we may have faced disappointments...
We may not know if we will see each other tomorrow...
But tonight, why don't we just forget everything and slow dance under the moonlight...

Shades of a Rainbow

Shades of pink
Shades of green
Shades of blue
Shades of yellow
Shades of orange
I am a rainbow.
But why does the world only prefer shades of grey from every individual?
And is skeptical when one showcases their inner colors of diversity?

Shades of Grey

Do not view life as black or white.
Have you ever thought of grey?
Grey is a color too and it's always there in the palette…
But you choose black or white.
We are grey.
We are people who make hay when the sun shines…
And do not bother whether the hay is good or bad,
Whether the yield is good or bad
We just make hay.
And think it's life's way…

Free Bird

I wish I could quit my job today and travel everywhere…
Where people would not question me
Whenever I go here and there…
I would roam around the earth like a free bird.
With no one at my lair…
But alas the new norm has different plans!
I did not go anywhere.
I did not quit my job…
But got fired, out of nowhere!
I can travel but with caution.
With sanitizer and temperature checks everywhere…
Pubs, cafes, and parks, every place has a checkpoint of beeping thermometer and oximeter…
I wished I could be a free bird…
But I am nothing but a masked bird,
With doctors and BBMP always at my lair!

I Have Come a Long Way

From being scared about what others will say...
From being scared about what others might think,
From thinking that others will judge me for my actions.
I have come a long way.

From not being able to express myself
From not being able to deal with my emotions,
From not being able to stop depending on others,
I have come a long way.

From not being able to get up from bed...
From not being able to stop being needy,
From not being able to stop pleasing others,
I have come a long way.

I have conquered my inhibitions.
I have conquered my fears.
I have set boundaries for myself and others…
I have built healthy relationships with myself and others...
But at times I feel vulnerable
At times there is a reappearance of overthinking and anxious behavior...
At times there is a slip, but I manage to recover…

Yes, in my journey of self-discovery,
I have come a long way.
I have crossed a bridge,
But I still have the ocean to cross!

What if Stars Could Speak?

Then they would say do not
Look up to us for the sparkle.
The sparkle is right within you and around you...
It lies in the twinkling eyes of every child, you see,
Who has millions of questions.
But you do not have answers...
The child whose sparkle you sometimes stifle
Because you do not have the answers... or just cannot answer?
This is how we kill the inner sparkle of the child within us...
And stop questioning,
Till the point where we search externally for a glimmer, or a shine maybe?
Do not stifle that inner child anymore.
Let the child sparkle and wreak havoc in the night sky.

Love Yourself

Love yourself, they say...
But when you do love yourself and do what you please...
Why do they question you?
Why do they tell you that your song is not worth listening to?
Let me tell you a secret...
If you truly love yourself...
You will not care about what they say...
But never forget that self-love...
When you beg someone to listen!

Why?

Why do we say we empathize?
When in fact no one really can...
For what I feel, you will never know...
And what you think, I will never know!
You can sympathize darling, but never empathize...

Cosmic Love

As he looked up above,
He sighed to her, oh so insignificant is our love in comparison with the cosmic world...
Perfectly true... so insignificant! She agreed...
And broke up with him the next day.

The Parting

I am tired, he said.
And I knew that the end was near.
The end of a period that felt like a roller coaster ride...
A period of bittersweet memories…
I did not know why but was relieved...
Relieved that it was the end...
Yet, it was a sad end...
End of a journey of friendship and understanding...
Alas! I wish it could have remained that way.
That I could be his friend and nothing more.
but the expectations were there, from both ends...
Expectations that were tiring us down…

Mirage

We see it from a distance
And try to reach out.
But forget it's not a mirror image,
It's a mirage.
Why do we believe in a mirage?
Why do we fall prey to make-believe?
Why do we believe in such an image which does not exist...
What is it that we look for?
What is it that we want,
that makes us susceptible to a mirage?
And believe it to be a true image of self.

Love, A Mirage

Is love a mirage too?
That exists during certain periods of time?
And is not there the rest of the time...
Is it a make-believe?
A false image that we create?
And convince ourselves that the mirage is there even when it's not there...
It's hard to tell...
Really hard to tell...

My Love

My love for you, though new, is beyond boundaries.
There may be days when you would want to lift me and kiss me…
And others where you might be baffled by my ridiculous behavior.
But just know though I may not always show,
My love for you is strong…
Right now, you are a strength, I am thankful for but scared to lean on
I hope I will be able to understand you the way you do…
I hope I would someday be a better person for you.

Thoughts on Love

I understand love a bit...
It's not only when one holds your hand...
But when they ask you,
Are you ok?

Take a Breath of Fresh Air

Take a breath of fresh air.
Relax, you are not in a lion's lair.
It's not that you will not die tomorrow.
But until then why not say goodbye to your sorrows?
Smile, it will brighten your day,
Who knows, it might stay all the way.
And help you to brave darkness strongly and not sway.
Why ask others to change when you know that everything, even
the change is temporary?
And after a while, it will be nothing but a memory: happy, sad, or grey.
It's for you to say...
Life is short, is cliché.
But it is true whatever you may say.
So just sing along to your favorite song and be merry as its
always not yours but life's way.

Freedom

Those who have freedom, don't recognize its worth.
those who don't, fight for it!
But where does it lie?
One's sense of freedom?
It's not limited or enhanced by
Materialistic boundaries or lines and demarcations...
It lies deep within our inner self.
Which defines our sense of self…

You

I think of you often
But am I ever in your thoughts?
Your smile gave you away.

Lilies Are Forever

Lilies are forever, they blossom in the spring or never.
But when they spring to life, they leave behind a mark that never leaves you altogether.
Just like my love towards you...
Which will stay forever?

Fixture

Changing times, changing me
Life changes in a blink of an eye
Cause' Aren't we all dancing to life's tunes?
But oh! There's one thing that won't change
And that's you
Because you are the fixture despite my changing hues
You are a fixture, who appreciates my every view.
You are the white who is omnipresent in my life's every hue.
Bringing a beacon of hope in me, that life will be beautiful with you.

Rain

Rain, you drift, you play with the wind...

I hold you; you escape from my fingertips...

You arrive suddenly, fall relentlessly,

I am astounded by your tactful way of bringing everyone to admire you... by bringing traffic to a standstill...

Now dear Bangalore rain, please do not laugh at my few unconnected lines...

I am just like you, not able to connect the entire city.

Drizzling in Jayanagar, but not in Indiranagar

Undecided me, undecided you

So, I invite you to a cup of tea at a rooftop cafe in Bangalore.

Words

Words, they break you.
Words, they make you.
Some comfort you ...
Some pierce you...
But you need them, and they need you...
Aren't life stories built on a cacophony of words?
Some word stories you weave, some life weaves it for you...
That is why maybe we are taught word-building when young!
To learn to build our life, through the words that decide our destiny ...

Dance

Dance to the tunes of life, some say...

But why not create your own tune and dance to your heart's content?

Moments

Never let go of those moments,
Moments that bring you boundless joy
So, what if it's just a moment?
It's these moments that make a lifetime.

The End

They said it's no good, let's put an end to it!
And in the end, they did...
Little did they realize the number of livelihoods they ended,
That later led to the end of many lives, of every age and gender.

A Gesture

A gesture so tender, that my heart went off its fender.
But little did I know that it was nothing but a gesture...
The sunset from the east and rose from the west that day!
And all of it was for nothing but a meaningless gesture that now seems lackluster...

Apoorva Ravi

She

A silent dove or a vocal lark—she maybe both, or none.
But the world is not aware …
Or maybe does not care?
Of the innocence reflected in every talk
The simplicity in her walk

They hear not when she cries,
They care not when she tries…
To make everything right
Or trying too hard to delight…

She is too difficult said some,
She is as plain as paper, said the other.
Perhaps she was both, perhaps none…

This is what she thinks, this is what she feels.
But it's sad that she's not aware…
That the world rejoices in her laughter
And always wipes her glistening tears.
But she is not aware, let us make her aware…

Amma

Her eyes were watery, and her face was sweaty, so I asked her about it...
But she said don't worry, it's nothing...
But the next day, she was right beside me when I was pacing up and down not having finished my deadline!
My friend during my best and my worst
A shield from all worries and woes
My sunshine during blistering cold
A cool gal during fun and jokes
She is my Amma, and I have known no one like her ever.
There need not be just a day, but every day is dedicated to you...

Imprints

Every step you take leads to an imprint on the way.
An imprint that's either frivolous or impactful you may say.
So, tread carefully some say...
But you my friends always do follow what your heart says...
The world is your canvas,
Do not think!
And just dance away.
And create the imprints of your little whims and fancies.
Of tiny moments that are just yours to play
For those that make life beautiful for you and the ones
around you.

Unseen Under the Moonlight

Half hidden, half seen,
Peeking through the curtain of clouds,
Is the nighttime wanderer, the moon...
The sole companion for lost travelers and star-crossed lovers maybe?

Oh dear, why not you join me today under the moonlight?
We will share the day's musings and our night-time yearnings.
We will remain unseen under the moonlight.

Let's Be Unconventional

A glass of Ferrero Rocher is beautiful, not when you gulp it, but when you relish it spoon by spoon.

A drop of rain is beautiful not when you sit and complain in the traffic jam, but when drops of it fall in the cup of tea you relish!

Do not just scroll down that photograph,

Take time to understand it,

Just as I ask you to not dismiss this as a mere verse,

But understand the hidden me behind!

Life is a Symphony

Life is a symphony of unforeseen moments.
Time is its sole composer
And we have to sing along
To make it a melody.

Saw Something Old

I saw something old but found something new.
Life shows us every day, a new hue in every dew.
Why not, you show me today, the hidden child in you…
Carefree and unhurried,
Joy some and unworried…

Travel is Better than Destination

Travel is better than a destination, moving from road to
road, point to point.
Nature is man's solace, answers his need to laze.
I am amidst this picturesque maze…
I did not know whether to dance or gaze…

Mindless Mirages

Walk through life, following symbolic images
By coming out of restricted cages
And not be distracted by mindless mirages.

The Breeze

Let go and be with the breeze
And it will take you wherever you please.

The Piano

I was playing the piano, and I fell asleep.
Was it the music that I played? Or the music in my ear?
Or perhaps it was the symphony that seemed like a lullaby,
And soothed the child in me …

The Wind Whispering in My Ear

The wind whispering in my ear,
A tune so beautiful that I sang it aloud…
But alas!
It's a tune you can never identify with…
Why should our tunes be so different?
When I say pop, you say classical.
Why don't you and I learn to play a harmonious melody?
A melody which we can sing to our friends and family?
But oh!
When you play the high note, I play the low…
It's not the classical or the pop that matters,
Our respective choices are not wrong,
They are just out of tune and out of sync when played together…
Indicating that we are two tunes that do not go together!

He Awakens in Me a Side

He awakens in me, a side that I know so little
A side that wants to be loved,
A side that desires to be nurtured
Why don't I let that side of me grow?
Why do I fear?
And not flow
With the emotions of love
That I fear to give him…
That I fear to give myself…
Why?
Why did the need to be independent clash with my desire to love?
Why can't I be me and be with him?
Why do I need to be without him, to be me?

Sometimes Life Needs No Music

Sometimes life needs no music.
Silence is music in itself…
The silence in every pause
The silence in every breath
The silence that resounds in my heart
Whenever I look towards the sky…
Reminding me that I am carefree and me.
Life does not always need music.
Sometimes, it's the silence that reminds us of what we are…
And what we want to be.

Familiarity in the Unfamiliar

Finding familiarity in the unfamiliar is what we humans do...
Dusting cobwebs off old books and inhaling the welcoming scent of paper,
Being pleasantly surprised by a known song in an unknown playlist.
Finding our favorite food comforting after experimenting with diverse palates.
Isn't it just the way I look for your familiar eyes to lock with, in a sea of unfamiliar faces?

It Is Not Over

It is not over,
It is not over when you feel that this is all that I can ever be.
It is not over when it seems that there is nothing in this world to be…
It is not over when you imagine the smiling sun as scorching heat.
It is not over when you believe, the cruel winter will always be.

Don't worry!
It is never over…
Even when you feel that your life is over.
For neither you nor I am aware of the tumultuous twists of fate…
There will be a turning paint.
When you will sway with joy along with the winter breeze
Smile back at the beaming sun,
Turn back to life and say, 'You were right! It is never over.'

Interlude

The chirping birds were flying by, eager to reach their homes,
At a speed that would have made any racer sigh, and yearn to follow them, if only he could fly…
The eagles began gliding in the sky, along with the bats that came by.
To claim the night sky as their own.

The sky's appearance seemed to change quietly, so as to not shock a passerby with its dramatic display,
The shifting clouds and the sun drifting behind them,
Made way for the shy moon, who would have happily stayed behind a cloud until noon…
But she didn't even know that she was the guiding light for many lost souls of the night!

Unconcerned about the activities around them, were four
parrots perched on a branch so high,
That no one could identify them with bare eyes...
As I gazed at them through my coveted lens,
I felt they were having a round table conference.
Fluttering their wings now and then, but not making a
single move to return to their den...

Suddenly I heard a loud cry of an eagle nearby,
Who descended on the same branch where the foursome
was having an interlude...
The branch was abandoned, their conference forgotten,
As they shot out into the night sky...
Shocking the unsuspecting eagle who had not seen the
parrots perched so high...
Leaving him to wonder, what had happened and why!

The Life of a Prisoner

I closed my eyes with gratitude,
As each drop fell on my face, cleansing my convoluted thoughts!
Each drop took away with it, every pain and suffering…
I wondered, rain is so beautiful.
It has healing powers, it has given me hope, and a new life.
I deeply regret the heinous crimes I have committed…
I am redeemed.

Oh! But these drops don't seem to stop.
I am feeling cold!
I think I will get up now, to face my new life.

I cannot move.
I am tied to a pole!
Can somebody please untie me?
No one seems to listen to me…
The drops continue to fall.
I am freezing, but no one is untying me.
I am not the same person, I have changed!

The same drops that gave me a new life now seemed intent
on torturing me…

The guard has come.
'Please release me,' I pleaded…
He is not listening to me!
He pushed a plate of food and is walking away.
Don't go! Please do not leave me, I have changed,
The guard turned back, to look at me,
He said, 'Perhaps you have changed, or perhaps not.'
'I don't care, nobody cares.'
'Once a sinner, always a sinner.'

About the Author

Apoorva is a writer, poet, and mental health advocate. With lived experience in the field of mental health, she wants to spread awareness in the field. She is a Gender Studies PhD scholar and has been a teacher for four years. She is also a music enthusiast and adores her cats and dog to bits.